TALE OF A CAT

*A Journal About
the Life & Good Times of
Your Feline Friend*

 _____

YOUR CAT'S NAME

*"If man could be crossed with the cat, it would improve man
but it would deteriorate the cat."*—**Mark Twain**

T A L E
O F A
C A T

Copyright 1995
Marlin Bree

Text and Illustrations by Marlin Bree
Poetry by Will Bree
Paw prints by Hing Bree

Published by Marlor Press, Inc.
All rights reserved.

ISBN 0-943400-82-1

Printed in the U.S.A

Distributed to the book trade by
Contemporary Books, Chicago

Disclaimer: *This book is intended only to impart broad general information in matters of cat ownership and feline behavior. It does not
replace specific instructions or guidelines concerned with safety, health
or feline welfare from veterinarians or other cat specialists. Pet owners
should use their own judgement to meet their pet's specific needs or
problems. For medical problems, or recurring behavioral problems, contact a veterinarian or other qualified pet specialist. In any event, Marlor Press, Inc. and the authors are not responsible for safety, services,
damages, loss, or injury of any kind.*

M A R L O R P R E S S , I N C .
4304 Brigadoon Drive / Saint Paul, MN./ 55126

DEDICATED
TO MY CAT

Picture

of

your cat

here

**As kept by cat's humble servant
and faithful friend**

_____

YOUR   NAME

_____

DATE

IMPORTANT

*In an emergency,
call this telephone number:*

_____

Telephone number of your cat's veterinarian or clinic

CONTENTS

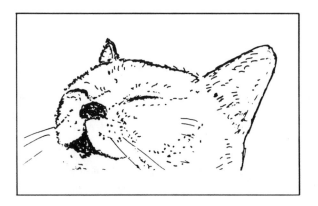

INTRODUCTION

Welcome to *The Tale of a Cat*. Specifically, the story of *your* cat.

As you author this book, you will see why your furry friend is not only a splendid individual—it seems no two cats are exactly alike—but a remarkable companion. Doing this will help you understand your cat better and make your life with your feline a little more comfortable and friendly.

It's easy to keep a fascinating record of your furry friend. There are some cat facts and cat fancies to keep you amused and informed as you progress through the book. Take your time.

Tale of a Cat will deepen the relationship between you and your cat. The book will help you create a wonderful treasury of moments and events in the life of your favorite feline. When you are finished, you can place this book on your library shelf as a memento.

You will have a tale of a cat as only you can keep it.

PAWS FOR THOUGHT

Cats rule supreme these days. There are about 62 million cats in the United States alone, vastly outnumbering the number two pet, dogs.

Various surveys show how wild we are about our cats:

- Most cat owners spend 45 minutes to an hour each day engaged in activities with their feline friends.

- Over half of all cat owners let their feline family members sleep in bed with them on a regular basis.

- About 40 percent of owners celebrate their cat's birthdays; some even send cards.

- Half give their cats presents at Christmas time.

- Most owners have a favorite nickname for their cats.

- Nine out of 10 owners talk to their cats.

- Some leave the television set on for their cats to watch.

- About 20 percent keep photos of their cats in their wallets

- Most owners feel that having a cat around the house reduces stress and keeps them mentally healthy.

As the surveys show, we are really crazy about our cats—and it's obviously a mutual attraction.

 How can you identify cats?
By looking at a cat-alog

Section 1:

♥ KITTEN TALES

A purr-sonal record of your kitten's first year

MY KITTEN

Paste

in

picture

of your kitten

and yourself

**One of the first pictures
of my kitten and me**

♥ _____
Date taken

♥ _____
Age of my kitten when the photo was taken

♥ MY KITTEN'S FULL NAME

_____

First name

_____

Middle name (If appropriate)

_____

Last name

_____

Nickname or nicknames

♥ My kitten came to live with me

_____

Day   Month   Year

At this age

_____

Months   Days

♥ My kitten is from the following place

_____

Name

_____

Street address

_____

City   State   Zip

_____

Telephone Number

_____

Person I dealt with

Type of cat

If your cat is pure bred, indicate breed. If not, just indicate types of breeds, if known, or American Domestic.

_____

♥ Fur color or colors

_____

_____

♥ Special markings

_____
Head
_____
Paws
_____
Tail

♥ Length

_____
Inches from nose to tip of tail

♥ Eye color or colors

_____

_____

    Why does a cat have fur?
Because it'd look silly in pajamas

☙ BACKGROUND

Give some information about your cat's background and
relatives, such as the mother's name, size of the litter,
where it was raised, etc. If your cat is a purebred,
you can add details of its purebred registration here:

_____

_____

_____

_____

_____

_____

_____

_____

_____

What do cats like on their hot dogs?
Cats-up

♥ ♥ ♥ KITTEN ♥ ♥
♥ ♥ ♥ MEMORIES ♥ ♥ ♥

♥ Our kitten was this long (including tail)
when he or she first arrived:

_____

Inches   and   fractions of an inch

♥ And this much of our kitten was tail:

_____

Inches   and   fractions of an inch

♥ His or her weight was:

_____

Ounces

♥ I picked this kitten because

_____

_____

♥   ♥   One of the first things the kitten did   ♥   ♥
  ♥   ♥   when it arrived home was: ♥   ♥

_____

_____

_____

_____

♥ Cute kitten tales to record for posterity:

_____

_____

_____

_____

♥   The kitten's favorite thing to do
          it should not have done:

_____

_____

_____

_____

♥   *What do cats like to do?*
          Take a cat-nap

KITTEN
FIRSTS

Your record of kitten's milestones
(such as its first time up the sofa.)

Date	Thing your kitten did

♥ ♥ If the kitten could talk, ♥ ♥ ♥
♥ ♥ its favorites would be ♥ ♥

Food

_____

_____

Favorite sleeping positions

_____

_____

Favorite places to be touched

_____

Favorite words or sounds

_____

_____

Favorite mischief

_____

_____

Best loved toy

_____

♥

♥ ♥ ♥   ♥ How my ♥   ♥   ♥   ♥
♥   ♥   ♥   kitten grew   ♥   ♥   ♥

Date	Age	Weight	Length

I have made up my mind that my cat
will _____ will not _____
sleep in bed with me.

My kitten thinks it
will _____ will not _____
honor my decision.

♥

Section 2

ABOUT
MY
BIG CAT

**My favorite
feline
grows up!**

MY CAT

Paste

in

picture

of your adult cat

and yourself

**A picture of
my adult cat and me**

Date taken

Age of my cat when the photo was taken

MY NICKNAMES FOR MY BIG CAT

_____
Nickname

_____
Nickname

My cat's adult fur color or colors

_____

_____

Special markings

_____
Head

_____
Paws

_____
Tail

My cat's adult length

 _____
Inches from nose to tip of tail

Eye color or colors

_____

_____

What kinds of cars do rich felines own?
Cat-illacs

FUR, FUR AWAY!

Paste samples of fur

you combed

from your cat here

THINGS MY
CAT LOVES

My cat's favorite place in the sun

_____

_____

Times my cat likes to play

_____

_____

Some foods my cat especially likes

_____

_____

My cat can sleep this long uninterrupted

_____

_____

My cat's favorite toys

_____

_____

_____

What goes meow and has two wheels?
Cat on a bicycle

WEIGHT   CHART

Date	Age	Pounds	Ounces	Over/Under*

*Weight over or under recommended target weight

PAWS FOR THE RECORD

You can acquire, with a little help from your feline friend, an actual paw print by using harmless food coloring. Spread blank papers on the floor, as well as lots of newspapers. Have your cat step onto a thin coating of food coloring in a flat dish, then walk across the papers. From several paw prints, you should be able to get a suitable one for posterity. Paste that above. Note: Be certain to have a warm washcloth handy to wipe off the colored paws. We've found it's handy to wipe them several times and have your cat walk around on the spread newspapers several times as well to be certain all the food coloring is gone.

A CURRENT PHOTOGRAPH

Paste

in a favorite

picture

of your

cat

About this photograph:

_____

_____

_____

_____

MILESTONES

Special events in your cat's life worthy of record

_____

_____

_____

_____

_____

_____

_____

_____

_____

_____

CAT FACTS AND FANCIES

The ancient Egyptians worshipped cats as gods. There was even a cat god, Bast, who had a temple where people could worship. This is a high point in feline history that your cat has never forgotten.

Cats were the last wild creatures to become domesticated.

Cats can easily recognize what their masters tell them, including their names and various commands. But that doesn't mean a cat has to do anything about it.

Cats are good at cat napping. This is because they are great hunters who have to store up lots of energy for quick bursts of activity. Apparently, this takes a lot of storing.

How much sleep does a cat really need? Experts say about 16 hours a day. Some cats sleep 24 hours a day—and seem to need even more.

Cats are independent. They will cooperate when they feel like it. They don't believe in doing things just because somebody else wants them to do it. You can check with your cat on this.

A cat, when fully grown, weighs six to twelve pounds. The heaviest cat on record was a tabby in Great Britain, who tipped the scales at a whopping 40 pounds.

Question: Where does a 40-pound cat sit?
Answer: Anywhere he wants!

Cats have unusual flexibility because their spine is not held together by ligaments, such as humans have, but by muscles. Cats also have 26 more vertebrae than man.

Cats are nature's great athletes. The key to their acrobatic skills is that they can use their tails as counterweights.

Cats can sprint short distances at speeds up to around 30 m.p.h. However, they don't want to do this very often as it takes a lot of effort.

Cats can't see in the dark but they can see at much lower levels of light than humans—one-sixth of the light level humans require. Cats can see color but it doesn't seem to mean much to them.

Cats have good memories. However, as most owners know, they often conveniently choose not to use them all the time.

HERE KITTY KITTY   ??? KITTY HERE

HOW TO PHOTOGRAPH YOUR CAT

1 / Let your cat become adjusted to your camera. Keep it around when you are near your furry friend.

2 / Don't shoot down on your cat; instead, try to be at your favorite feline's eye level. Lower yourself physically or else get your cat up on a shelf or a table.

3 /Enjoy yourself. Have a good time taking pictures of your cat. Your cat will sense your mood—it will show.

4 / You can make your cat appear more alert by playing a few minutes with it and having a favorite toy near. That special look of interest that professional photographers capture is sometimes provided by a cat toy suspended near a cat's head.

5 / Move up close. Remember that your cat is small. Have your cat's image fill your viewfinder. A good picture is just of your cat's head and the top of its body.

6 / Don't shoot your cat with the light behind it or with the sun directly overhead. Morning or late afternoon, when the sun's rays are more horizontal, are best for lighting your cat. Shade is good, too.

7 / Be ready to shoot a lot of pictures. Film is inexpensive. If you have a 35mm camera, you can devote an entire role of film to get that one perfect shot.

8 / Don't bore your cat. When it is tired of being photographed, *stop*. You can always resume again at a later time when your fuzzy friend lets you know it is ready.

Spinal stretch by the morning,
Spy the domain over which you're lording.
Ignominiously caught with sides heaving:
Perhaps it was time to be leaving.—WB

Section 3:

A
CAT'S
JOURNAL

**A record of fun,
happenings,
and good times
in your cat's life**

A CAT'S JOURNAL

A record of fun, happenings,
and good times in your cat's life

_____

_____

_____

_____

_____

_____

_____

_____

_____

_____

_____

_____

_____

I am a devout feline,
Trustworthy, loyal and stable.
Now, will you kindly leave me alone
With that chicken on the table?—WB

THE CAT WITH
SOX APPEAL

He had been abandoned in Little Rock, Arkansas, and adopted by a piano teacher. When Mrs. Clinton and Chelsea visited the piano teacher for Chelsea's lesson, they fell in love with the cat and the teacher gave the cat to Chelsea. Because of his white paws, he acquired the name Socks.

From these humble beginnings, Socks became the first cat in over a decade to occupy the White House as the pet of President Bill Clinton, First Lady Hillary Rodham Clinton, and daughter Chelsea. Socks achieved celebrityhood and inspired a number of "socks appeal" items such as t-shirts, bumper stickers, and Socks look-alike stuffed cats. On the average, the Post Office counted about 25 letters a month addressed to the cat at the White House. Socks even inspired his own Socks the Cat Fan Club.

Socks was the first Tuxedo Cat in the White House. The previous feline occupiers of the White house were purebred Siamese Cats, Misty Malarky Ying Yang, owned by Amy Carter, and before the Carters, there was Shan, the Gerald Ford family cat.

How long do cats like to stay in the White House?
Fur a long time!

A CAT'S JOURNAL

A record of fun, happenings,
and good times in your cat's life

_____

_____

_____

_____

_____

_____

_____

_____

_____

_____

_____

_____

_____

Are cats wealthy?
No, most are purr!

A CAT'S JOURNAL

A record of fun, happenings,
and good times in your cat's life

_____

_____

_____

_____

_____

_____

_____

_____

_____

_____

_____

In ancient times, humans worshiped the feline race,
Believing from the heavens cats did descend.
Though we from the ancients have turned our face,
In the minds of cats it never came to an end.—WB

A CAT'S IDEAL ROOM

(According to the cat)

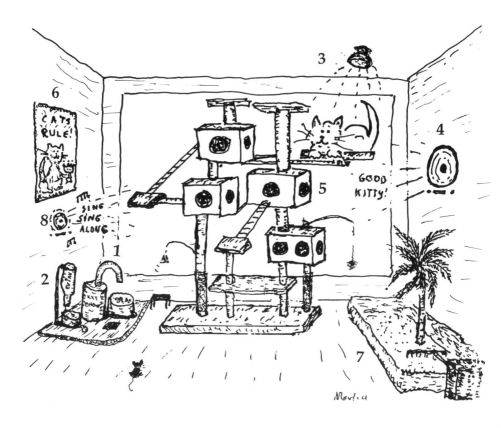

Cats have special needs, as any cat will tell you, including a room to themselves. Here is plan for a space designed to keep your cat happy—at last.

1 Perpetual ever-full cat chow feeder, guaranteed *never* to greet your cat with an empty bowl just when your feline so desperately needs that midnight snack.

2 Water bowl filled with imported spring water and emptied on the hour so that it is always fresh. *Yum.*

3 Eternal warmth and sunshine for your favorite feline with an electronic sun lamp. Mr. Happy Sunbeam is also good to sleep under whenever your cat needs a little cat nap, which is often.

4 Recorded *Warm Voice* from the Great Cat Master in the Sky to reassure your cat in dulcet tones that he or she is tops. Includes the ever-inspiring *What a nice kitty.*

5 A decent-sized climbing tree and scratching post. Complete with split-level kitty habitats and attached action toys.

6 A tasteful poster to keep your cat's morale up and to help remind your feline of his or her regal heritage furr-ever.

7 A Sahara-sized kitty litter pan with an automatic changer after every use so your cat's paws will always feel dainty fresh. Purr-fect for every feline.

8 *Cats Sing Along* for whenever your cat feels like a singing session over the (simulated) backyard fence. Includes caterwauling harmony on such feline favorites as *Broadway Kitten, Old Garrison's Cat, and Catnip of My Dreams.* Also available: the recording from the hit show, *Katz,* featuring the original Broadway feline cast.

A CAT'S JOURNAL

A record of fun, happenings,
and good times in your cat's life

_Please do not drink
the milk at the table.
You are welcome to sit,
but refrain if you're able.
I would not have it said,
that I am unwilling to share;
But I've seen where you wash,
when you groom your hair._—WB

A CAT'S JOURNAL

A record of fun, happenings,
and good times in your cat's life

_____

_____

_____

_____

_____

_____

_____

_____

_____

_____

_____

_____

_____

_____

*A good morning's stretch
on a warm winter's night,
leaves one ready to break
and sleep till light*

*With the coming of morn,
a bright sky does itself lend;
To curling back up,
and returning to sleep again.—*WB

▼▼▼▼▼▼▼▼▼▼▼▼▼▼

A CAT'S JOURNAL

A record of fun, happenings,
and good times in your cat's life

_____

_____

_____

_____

_____

_____

_____

_____

_____

_____

_____

_____

_____

_____

Do not disturb your sleeping cat,
though his slumbers grow long
or his belly fat.
Leave him alone, for goodness sake,
he is grumpy enough when awake.—WB

▼▼▼▼▼▼▼▼▼▼▼▼▼▼▼

A CAT'S JOURNAL

A record of fun, happenings, and good times in your cat's life

_____

_____

_____

_____

*The gift of the cat
is not to land on all four feet;
Instead, it is to land
on all four feet---and live!*—WB

_____

_____

_____

_____

_____

_____

_____

C A T S
A T
S E A

Ancient mariners carefully studied a cat's gestures, movements, and even attitudes to try to foretell not only good luck but weather or future problems at sea.

If a ship's cat, for example, licked its paws or its tail, this was thought to mean rain. A cat's sneeze meant the same thing. If it licked its fur the wrong way, that meant the ship was headed for bad luck. If the feline washed itself normally and slept with the back of its head down, good weather lay ahead.

Superstitious sailors thought that cats had certain powers over the wind. If the animal clawed a bunk, piece of furniture or scratched a rug, then it was thought to be attempting to raise a wind. If the cat switched its tail angrily, that meant gale-force winds were headed toward the ship. If it played with a string, lanyard, or a rope, that meant the cat was trying to raise a storm. A cat mewing at night was thought to be summoning a tempest. Beware the cat climbing the rigging: the ship was doomed!

Cats contributed to the language of the sea. There was, for example, the scourge of the cat-o-nine-tails, which was a whip with nine "tails"; weak drinks were called cat-lap, and a sailor's quick doze was called, what else, but a cat nap.

How do cats like to travel?
Fur

A CAT'S JOURNAL

A record of fun, happenings,
and good times in your cat's life

_____

_____

_____

_____

_____

_____

_____

_____

_____

_____

_____

Too late he understood, too late he arose;
Too late he discovered the significance
Of that squatting pose.—WB

A CAT'S JOURNAL

A record of fun, happenings, and good times in your cat's life

_____

_____

_____

_____

_____

_____

_____

_____

_____

_____

I apologize profusely,
Your squalling was most apt.
I should have been watching
Where it was I sat.—WB

Section 4:

FUN
& GAMES
WITH
YOUR CAT

Cat toys you can make
and some training tips
for your cat (shh!)

 CAT TOYS YOU CAN MAKE

**And some tips on
how to play
with your cat**

Approach playtime with a fun attitude. You'd be surprised at how quickly your feline can sense your mood.

A little talk with your cat as you present a toy also will help. Your pet won't understand your words but is an absolute demon on picking up the sense of what you are saying.

Make your moves small, abrupt and light. The idea is to arouse your cat's interest, as if you were presenting it with something from the wild to pounce upon.

Move your toy about so that your pet gets some good exercise leaping, batting, and slinking. If it stops playing, but merely lays there awaiting your next move, your cat may be training you to bring the "prey" to it.

Sometimes it's helpful if you simply stop your play and

wait, holding the toy still. Few cats can resist a rapidly moving object that suddenly stops moving. This is when you'll see your cat's eyes grow wide, its rear switch back and forth, and your pet will pounce.

Play until your cat shows some signs of tiring, but is still interested. Then put the toys away. Your cat will find them intriguing all over again next time.

Catch the "tail"

Mother cats use their tails to teach kittens how to chase and pounce on prey. A string or piece of yarn—which reminds a cat of mother's tail—makes a good toy for a cat.

Most any type of string, yarn, or light rope will do, but for a variation, tie the end of the string to a stick or a fiberglass pole. This can give the "tail" a little extra movement.

To the end of the string, you also can tie or attach a piece of cloth, a bit of leather, or a cat toy. Jiggle the pole and make the toy dance; you can entice your cat to jump at it, bat it endlessly, and even do an occasional somersault.

Another trick is to move the toy across the floor and onto a couch and watch your feline friend do a slinky-stalking routine. Moving the string with item attached back and forth on a couch produces a special flurry of excitement.

If you attach a favorite toy to a string, you can also tie a rubber band between the toy and the string, suspend it at about eye level, and watch your cat bat this new toy about. You can experiment with different heights to see which one your cat likes best.

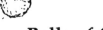

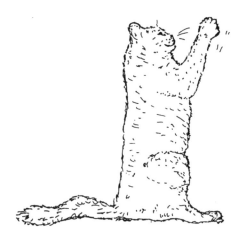

Balls of fun!

Ping-pong balls make great moving targets because cats can bat them about, chase them, and catch them.

Get your pet started by rolling a ping pong ball toward it. Or, if you stand in a hallway, some cats will actually bat the ball back toward you. For variety, gently bounce the ball just over your cat's head, against a wall.

Paper bag

Entertainment for hours can be had by opening up a brown paper bag, the kind you bring groceries in. Lay it on its side and watch your cat explore this new "cave."

After gaining some experience with it, your cat may even find that it's fun to run and dive into the bag—and watch it slide across the floor.

An alternative is to cut a small hole in one end of the bag and insert a small twig or stick. When you rattle this about, your cat will pounce! Some cat owners use a finger, but you'd better know your cat pretty well for this—or be quick. *(Note: Never use a plastic bag! It's dangerous for your pet and not as much fun.)*

In - Out

Draw a picture of a cat
and cut it out on cardboard or on wood or plywood. Letter
a sign that says "in" on one side and "out" on the other. Put
a loop on it so that you can hang it on the door or even
over the doorknob. When the cat goes outside, turn the cat
"out" sign outward so that everyone in the family can tell
where the cat is.

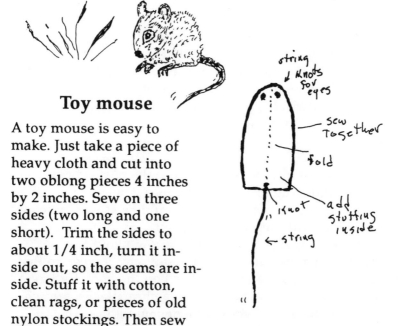

Toy mouse

A toy mouse is easy to
make. Just take a piece of
heavy cloth and cut into
two oblong pieces 4 inches
by 2 inches. Sew on three
sides (two long and one
short). Trim the sides to
about 1/4 inch, turn it inside out, so the seams are inside. Stuff it with cotton,
clean rags, or pieces of old
nylon stockings. Then sew
the short end shut, trapping the stuffing inside. You can
make it into a special treat by enclosing a small amount of
catnip in the stuffing.

Scratching post

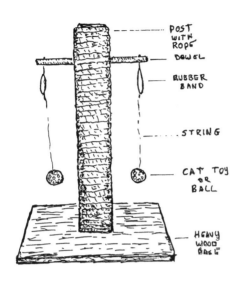

POST WITH ROPE

DOWEL

RUBBER BAND

STRING

CAT TOY OR BALL

HEAVY WOOD BASE

You can easily make a scratching post for your cat. Take a piece of wood, such as a 4 x 4 section, screw or nail that firmly to a base of plywood, and then cover it with a scrap of carpet. If you do not have extra carpet, you can go to a carpet store and get a small remnant or scrap. You can also cover the post with a rough rope wound around it.

Scratching posts can be straight forward or fancy. The main thing is that they should be appealing to the cat. Posts should be solid enough so that they do not tip over when used, so they will need a heavy, strong base. They should be high enough so that a cat can really reach up and stretch itself while it scratches. Some pet owners also sprinkle some catnip on the post to attract their favorite felines.

The best time to introduce your cat to the post is before there is a scratching problem. That means when you bring your cat home, a scratching post should be as available to your cat as its kitty litter pan and you should introduce your cat to both. Cat claws, as they grow, should be trimmed with a cat nail trimmer about once a week so that the cat doesn't have to work so hard on the post. If there are several areas where your cat scratches, place a scratching post nearby. Praise your cat whenever it uses the approved scratching post. Note: Even cats that have been declawed will instinctively need to scratch with their paws, so a scratching post is still a good idea.

Actor cats get what award?
A-cat-emy awards

COPING
WITH
YOUR
CAT

And letting your cat
cope with you

Even well-behaved cats sometimes develop behavioral problems, but experts believe that most cats can be trained with leadership, kindness, and understanding.

Physical punishment of your cat actually works against you. Do not run toward your cat yelling and waving your arms. This will not help train your cat and will only establish you as a "bad" person. What you want to do is turn the tables so that your cat's actions will have consequences the cat does not like while you remain the "good" person.

Try not to catch your cat doing something wrong; catch him or her doing something right. Then give your cat lots of eye contact and warm verbal praise. Cats love to be looked at and be talked to. If you work with your cat and motivate your furry friend, he or she will respond and try to please you. Sooner or later.

Writing down your cat's behavioral problems will help lead you to a solution. It's likely that you cat is giving you a lot of valuable clues. You need to observe the problem, write it down, and then define the situation. You want to understand why your cat is doing what it's doing. Early detection helps.

My cat's
behavioral
problems

Date   Problem

_____

_____

_____

_____

_____

_____

_____

_____

_____

_____

_____

_____

_____

_____

_____

_____

F *riendly*
E *njoyably, companionable*   _____
L *ovely, lovely, leonine*
I *nteresting, intellectually inquisitive.*   _____
N *ot to be trusted,*
E *ver!* —*WB*   ♥   _____

Problems and solutions

1/ My cat urinates or sprays on walls or furniture legs

Two things you can do are to put up aluminum foil to deflect the stream back, or, lay down packaging tape, sticky side up, which will stick to your cat's paws. Neither of these will make your cat happy. Clean the spritzed area immediately with a pet odor and stain remover.

2/ My cat sometimes does not use the kitty litter pan

Clean the litter box daily and be certain to refill it with the brand of litter your cat likes. Cats are very sensitive to smelly litter. Change not only the litter but wash the plastic litter pan. Your cat will soon return to its happier habits. If your cat seems not to get the idea, you can isolate your furry friend with the pan in a separate room until the your pet gets the habit again. Note: a urinary tract infection may be the cause of random urination, so if it continues, see your veterinarian.

3/ My cat returns to the same area to urinate or to spray.

Break the routine. Eliminate the spot with pet odor and stain remover. Use sticky tape or aluminum foil (#1 above)

4/ My cat likes to eat indoor plants

Put sticky tape near the plant or wrap foil around it. You can also keep a spray bottle of water handy. When the cat is eating your plant, spritz it from behind. In this way, the cat will link getting wet with eating the plant (never with

being punished by a beloved master.) Hint: grow some
greens especially for your cat. There are kits available
through pet stores which contain commercial grass seed,
growing mediums, and pots. You also can grow a natural
treat for your cat by putting some soil in a small plastic
dish such as a butter tub, punching holes in the bottom, ad-
ding some barley seeds and watering.

5/ My cat likes to jump on top the dining room table

Don't yell at the cat, pick it up and throw it off. All you are
doing is identifying yourself as a mean person. What you
want is to have the cat's own actions result in unpleasant
consequences so that your pet doesn't jump up on your
table. One way to do this is to put some tape with its sticky
side up on the table top. If you have ever seen a cat deal-
ing with sticky tape on its paws you will know that this is
an object lesson that will not have to be repeated often. In
the meantime, you are the good person to your feline
friend.. It's the cat's own action that caused the problem,
and you, beloved owner, had nothing to do with it. Cats
learn fast.

6/ My cat scratches the leg of my chair.

Introduce your cat to its own nearby scratching post so
that it can scratch there, instead of your furniture. You can
make your own inexpensive scratching post (see Fun &
games section) or you can buy one at a pet store. Ideally,
you should have a number around so that whenever kitty
gets the mood to scratch, there are posts handy and the cat
has a "safe scratching" area. Posts should be as close to the
former scratching area as possible.

You first will need to introduce your cat to its scratching
post, and as always, the best way to train a cat is through
play. Take a favorite toy, such as a mouse on a string, and
let the cat dig its claws into the post as it goes after the toy.
Work the toy around and above the post, so that your

feline friend gets the feel of the post and realizes how good it is. Praise your cat. Do this several times a day.

In the meantime, unpleasant consequences can occur if the cat should return to the leg of the chair. You can temporarily wrap the leg with sticky tape, or surround the leg with mousetraps, set under paper, so that when your pet approaches the leg, the mousetraps will go off with a loud snap. The paper will prevent any damage, but the noise will be shocking to the would-be scratcher.

7/ *My cat scratches my bedroom door at night, wanting in. I let her in, but then she wants back out. What's going on?*

Your cat wants attention, not in or out, and your furry friend is getting it. You need to train your cat, not allow your cat to train you. Put your feline friend in one room with a closed door, and if she scratches, don't get up to let her out. In fact, don't give her any notice at all. Yelling at her to stop only reinforces the behavior since it only provides a different form of attention. Keep toys in this room, a litter pan, and a scratching post. If she persists on scratching on the door to get your attention, you can make it unpleasant for her to do so while you remain the good person. Several things have worked: some sticky packaging tape, gummy side out will make her paws stick to the door (unpleasant!). You have to make the rules at night, not your cat.

8/ *My cat insists on going out-of-doors*

Cats do not have to leave the house or apartment. Many contented felines have lived their entire lives without going out-of-doors, which is dangerous to them and can cause many problems for their owners.

Training begins during kittenhood. Don't let your cat out of doors when it is young. Cats have to learn how nice it is to roll in the grass; do not give them this opportunity, no matter how kind it seems. Denying a feline access to the outside is the first step in the creation of an indoor cat. If, however, your feline companion has caught the love of nature, yearns for the outside, and dashes madly from your door, you have a major retraining program to launch.

Make it unpleasant for the cat to be outside. You, as your cat's boon companion, of course, will have nothing to do with this. One method is to lurk unseen to one side of an open door and squirt the cat with a water pistol or douse it with a partial pail of water the moment it steps out.

The soaked cat, shaking its wet head, will return to the comparative safety of the house. It may take a few wettings to discourage the cat's interests in the outdoors, but persistence, as always, will pay off.

NINE LIVES

One life to fill with sun,
a second to relive battles won;
The third to forget those he lost,
the fourth to pay that final cost.
A fifth, for every cost has tax,
And with the cost paid, the sixth to relax.
The seventh to savor by and by,
another to spend on wicked lie.
The last is saved for a fresh spring day,
and with all spent to
grin
and
fade
a
way...
—WB

Problems and solutions for my cat:

Date _____ Problem _____

_____

Solution to problem _____

_____

_____

_____

Date _____ Problem _____

_____

Solution to problem _____

_____

_____

_____

Date _____ Problem _____

_____

Solution to problem _____

_____

I must protest!
Desist, or face my wrath!
I most certainly do not need
A quick midwinter's bath! —WB

Date _____ Problem _____

_____

Solution to problem _____

_____

_____

_____

Date _____ Problem _____

_____

Solution to problem _____

_____

_____

_____

Date _____ Problem _____

_____

Solution to problem _____

_____

_____

_____

 Oh, joyous are my eyes.
Please ignore my tail.
It has absolutely nothing to do
With Colonel Sanders or that pail. —WB

TELL
TALE
TAILS

Your cat's tail is a part of its spine—actually about 1/3—and not only gives your pet maneuverability and equilibrium, but it can tell you a lot about what your favorite feline is thinking or doing.

Each cat has its own tail parlance. By careful observation, you can learn some important body language clues.

Little tail flicks indicate irritation; big sweeping motions, including thumping or lashing from side to side, mean the cat is aggressive or angry.

A fluffed out tail is a dramatic, but defensive gesture. It can deceive an opponent (look at the size of that beast!) by making the feline appear to be bigger and stronger than it actually is.

The cat's classic fighting stance is a tail carried low, bristling, and switching to and fro, teeth bared, ears flattened, while growling and spitting. It moves low to the ground, poised to strike, its body turned at an angle toward the perceived attacker.

The owner gives orders to the cat.
The cat gives orders to its tail. — Old folk saying

Sometimes, cats show their intentions first with their tails. A bristly, upright tail means the animal will fight, if necessary. But it also means that it is giving a fair warning— and offering to stage a mutual withdrawal without loss of dignity.

A cat moving toward you with its tail held high and an alert expression means it is glad to greet you. This can be accompanied by welcome meows, purrs, and, even an ingratiating stretch.

A cat usually carries its tail at a slight elevation to its body when walking. It may flick the tail from side to side, sometimes out of impatience. When it runs, the tail streams out behind and helps the feline balance itself while making those marvelous turns and jumps.

In an "attack" on a mouse or a toy, the cat will use a "slinking run," in which its body is close to the ground, its legs seeming to spin rapidly below, while the tail is held low but under tension. This slink-run lets the attacker remain close to the ground and, hopefully, unobserved by the prey.

A cat will signal it is going to charge by putting its tail up and switching powerfully from side to side. Sometimes the cat will also move its haunches.

Cats may end up "tail first" when they nestle in your lap. This is the way it acted as a kitten toward its mother when it presented its bottom for general looking over and for possible cleaning. Actually, this "bottoms up" approach is your pet's form of etiquette to you and a demonstration of its trust and love.

A tail held high, rather proudly, means the cat is feeling very good. On the other hand, a cat with its tail tucked in close behind its hind quarters means it is in poor spirits or wants to be left alone.

Some cats indicate their displeasure, or even their impudence, by flicking their tails---a feline version of thumbing one's nose.

Cats chase their tails for a variety of reasons. A mother cat wants her kittens to chase her tail as a way of teaching them balancing, chasing and hunting skills. Kittens chase each others' tails for fun and to acquire more athletic skills, related to hunting. They chase strings as an imitation of chasing their mother's tails.

Cats with their tails wrapped around their noses intend to have a good snooze. Actually, the tail helps reduce oxygen intake and helps produce a deep sleep. As they dream, they may make little noises or mutter in their sleep, and their tail ends may flick a bit.

In all, a cat's tail has quite a tale to tell.

Emerald eyes and curving tail,
quick of temper slow to fail.
With scything jaws, and wicked grin
quick-lived life, full of sin.
He stands alone while others pale.

—WB

GIFTS TO MY CAT

Many cat owners give presents to their cats for Christmas (about 50 percent) and for birthdays (40 percent). Here you can keep a record of what you give to your cat and when.

Date	Observance	Present

What town is not healthy for felines?
Curios-city

MY
CAT'S
SITTER

Many cat owners have a special
"catsitter" (or two)
to take care of their feline friend
when they are away.
Here is a handy record.

1/ Catsitter's name

Address

City   State   Zip

Telephone (s)

Helpful information

2/ Catsitter's name

Address

City   State   Zip

Telephone (s)

Helpful information

HELLO, CAT SITTER!

Information for our cat sitter.

(You can machine copy this)

Cat's name _____ Age _____

Special instructions

Feeding schedule _____

_____

Location of cat's food _____

Kitty litter instructions _____

Playing instructions _____

Other instructions: _____

_____

I can be reached at

Telephone number _____

Where I'll be _____

_____

My cat's veterinarian

Name _____

Clinic _____

Telephone _____

Emergency telephone _____

 Why are cats good storytellers?
Because of their tall tails

THAT DRAT MOLLY IVINS' CAT

It was in the Minneapolis Tribune's newsroom that I made a discovery: reporter Molly Ivins* had a cardboard box on her desk. That was how I first met Claudius, also called Clyde. The tiny gray kitten climbed out of the box as I put my face down. He bit me. Molly looked encouraged. "You want a kitten?" she asked.

I shook my head, no. What would I do with another cat? Ha! Later that day, the question became: what would I do with a kitten in a busy metropolitan daily newsroom? The answer was to put Clyde in the partially opened drawer in my desk. When I put my hand in, and left it there for a while, he would go to sleep. On the way home, in rush-hour traffic, he came awake and playful. I put him in my lap but he countered by crawling up through my coat sleeve to come to rest on my neck, where he mewed in my ear and gazed out on traffic.

I became aware that Clyde was going to be a special cat. He grew up to be long, gray and sleek. Fast, too, especially when he wanted to go outside. Over the years, he perfected the "Clyde bankshot" whereby if one looked about for the cat before opening a door, one would not see a cat. But when the door opened just a bit, there would be a scramble of paws, a furry bank shot off a nearby piece of furniture, and Clyde would be out! It was a masterful display of timing and agility.

*Molly Ivins went on to become a famous Texas newspaper columnist and best-selling author of Molly Ivins Can't Say That, Can She?

He was quick and graceful when he wanted to be. But
sometimes he was a loveable klutz. "Oh, what a beautiful
cat," a guest said during a dinner party as he proudly
strolled toward us. We all paused to admire Clyde, his
noble head and tail held high. When he passed beneath the
dinner table, we heard a disconcerting "thunk" noise. "I
think your cat just walked into the table leg," the guest
said apologetically. I looked below; there was Clyde, shaking his head.

After Clyde was several years old, we brought a Shetland
Sheepdog puppy into our home. Angus was a little ball of
fur, wobbly on his pins, and he eagerly wanted to make
friends with Clyde. Angus was a puppy, but Clyde, the
king of the household, was willing to be sociable if the little Sheltie knew his place. Whenever the pup would come
around to play, Clyde would place a large paw on Angus's
forehead and flatten the rolly polly guy to the carpet. Then
he would bathe his face with his tongue.When Angus grew
into an oversized Sheltie, he retained his love of the game
Clyde had taught him. Angus had also become very good
with his paws. He would come up to Clyde and place a
large, hairy paw upon the cat's head, flattening him. "Flat
cat" became a popular game for Angus, much to Clyde's
chagrin. Clyde resented the Sheltie baths, too.

Clyde was very athletic, but we always wondered how
he managed to get to the high rafters of our car
garage. One day I watched him take a long run across the
garage floor, jump about three-fourths of the way up on
one wall. He seemed to hang in mid-air for a milli-second.
Then his powerful hind quarters gave a big kick and he
flew straight upward until he was on top of the world.
How he learned how to do this I did not know. I was glad
not to have witnessed his practice sessions.

Later, when he chose to re-enter the garage, he somehow
forgot how to get back to the ground. I heard a pitiful
mewing, and there in the rafters was our great gymnastic

cat, his eyes focussed pleadingly on the floor. I had to coax him down, patting with my hands a preferred route to a shelf, then a box, and then the floor. He then made the small jumps down and came over for a pat for his great performance. This was so much fun that he repeated the performance again and again.

We live not far from a wooded area, above a small lake. Clyde discovered he was a hunter and loved nights in the wild. Days, too, if he could get them. He'd usually make it past us to go outside, using his bankshot when somebody arrived at the door, and then he'd stay out on a spree. We knew he was out there, though. When I opened the patio door in the morning, a dead mouse, or a part of one, greeted me. His gift to us.

Old age finally halted the long jumps and the woodsy rambles. He slept most of the day, and, toward the end, made a lot of visits with us to the vet, much to his distress. He had an incurable problem of failing kidneys and his remaining days were in misery. We made the inevitable final arrangements a merciful pet partner should arrange.

At the appointed time, my son, Will and I took him in, with Clyde nestled in Will's arms. When the needle was inserted, we stood around with our hands on our great feline friend, tears in our eyes. As he sank away from us, heading for the great feline in the sky, he again surprised us. He began purring.

---Marlin Bree

The dust begins to cover,
his quiet back trails.
No words can describe,
all attempts fail.
This space will never to be filled,
simple as that,
A void in my heart,
in the shape of a cat....—WB

KITTEN RECORD

Date of litter _____ Mother's name _____

Father's name _____ Number of kittens _____

	Kitten name	**Description**
1/		
2/		
3/		
4/		
5/		
6/		
7/		
8/		
9/		

🐾 NOTES

_____

_____

_____

_____

KITTENS WENT TO

1/
_____

Kitten name   Name of recipient

_____

Street address

_____

City   State   Zip

2/
_____

Kitten name   Name of recipient

_____

Street address

_____

City   State   Zip

3/
_____

Kitten name   Name of recipient

_____

Street address

_____

City   State   Zip

4/
_____

Kitten name   Name of recipient

_____

Street address

_____

City   State   Zip

5/
_____

Kitten name   Name of recipient

_____

Street address

_____

City   State   Zip

6/ _____

        Kitten name   Name of recipient

_____

                Street address

_____

     City   State   Zip

7/ _____

        Kitten name   Name of recipient

_____

                Street address

_____

     City   State   Zip

8/ _____

        Kitten name   Name of recipient

_____

                Street address

_____

     City   State   Zip

9/ _____

        Kitten name   Name of recipient

_____

                Street address

_____

     City   State   Zip

🐾 NOTES

_____

_____

_____

_____

Helpful hint: *For future litters, you can make
a machine copy of this record and staple it inside the back cover.*

Section 5:

YOUR
CAT'S
HEALTH

Your record of your cat's problems, illnesses, and visits to the vet

Note: Be certain to write down and keep handy emergency telephone numbers !

YOUR CAT'S VETERINARIAN

_____

Name of primary veterinarian

_____

Veterinarian's telephone number or numbers

_____

Emergency after-hours telephone number

Veterinarian clinic

_____

Name of clinic where your cat's vet practices

_____

Street address of clinic

_____

City   State   Zip

Clinic telephones

_____

Clinic's daytime phone number

_____

Clinic's *after hours* phone number for standby vet or emergencies

Directions to clinic:

_____

Clinic hours

_____

_____

Alternative veterinarian

_____
Name

_____
Specialty (if appropriate)

_____
Telephone number or numbers

_____
Emergency after-hours telephone number

Alternative clinic

_____
Name

_____
Street address

_____
City   State   Zip

_____
Daytime phone number

_____
After hours emergency telephone number

Record of your cat's visits to the vet

You can use the next pages as an appointment book, a record of your cat's problems, and, especially, as a written record of what transpired when you took your feline in for an appointment or an examination.

Write down the appointment in the **Time** and **Date** space. You already should have the vet's name, clinic name, and telephone numbers in the preceding pages.

Before you call for an appointment, you should jot down a few words about what you observe about your pet's illness, ailment or other problem. **Observed cat's problems** will be helpful when you meet your vet and explain your pet's needs.

What the vet did is a place to record the care the vet gave your cat. **What the veterinarian said** is where you record what the veterinarian tells you about your cat's condition and his diagnosis.

Under **Recommendations**, you can write down the vet's suggestions or other useful information.

You'll find a written record useful. For most people, it's difficult to remember verbal information accurately or for very long. Writing a few words down as your veterinarian talks to you will not only help you retain and use that important information, but it will let you compile a useful history of your cat's health problems.

 How does the store sell cat food?
It goes for so much purr sack

APPOINTMENT SCHEDULE

Time _____ Date _____

Veterinarian's name: _____

Observed cat's problem:

_____

_____

_____

What the veterinarian did:

_____

_____

What the veterinarian said:

_____

_____

_____

Recommendations:

_____

_____

_____

_____

Why couldn't the cat catch its tail?
Because it's difficult to make ends meet these days

A P P O I N T M E N T   S C H E D U L E

Time _____ Date _____

Veterinarian's name: _____

Observed cat's problem:

_____

_____

_____

What the veterinarian did:

_____

_____

What the veterinarian said:

_____

_____

_____

Recommendations:

_____

_____

_____

_____

_____

What's a great downpurr?
When it rains cats and dogs

APPOINTMENT SCHEDULE

Time _____ Date _____

Veterinarian's name: _____

Observed cat's problem:

_____

_____

_____

What the veterinarian did:

_____

_____

What the veterinarian said:

_____

_____

_____

Recommendations:

_____

_____

_____

_____

_____

What kind of coffee do cats like best?
Purr-colated coffee

APPOINTMENT SCHEDULE

Time _____   Date _____

Veterinarian's name: _____

Observed cat's problem:

_____

_____

_____

 What the veterinarian did:

_____

_____

What the veterinarian said:

_____

_____

_____

Recommendations:

_____

_____

_____

_____

APPOINTMENT SCHEDULE

Time _____ Date _____

Veterina ian's name: _____

Observed cat's problem:

_____

_____

_____

What the veterinarian did:

_____

_____

What the veterinarian said:

_____

_____

_____

Recommendations:

_____

_____

_____

_____

_____

CAT SIGNS

CATS RULE!

Have you hugged your cat today?

Cats are purr-fect pets

HONK if you love CATS

Never mind the cat. Watch out for the OWNER!

I'm a ♥ cat ADDICT

MEOW NOW!

I ♥ CATS

CAT CITY

BEWARE! Guard cat on duty

More cats less worry!

♥   APPOINTMENT SCHEDULE   ♥

Time _____ Date _____

Veterinarian's name: _____

Observed cat's problem:

_____

_____

_____

What the veterinarian did:

_____

_____

What the veterinarian said:

_____

_____

_____

Recommendations:

_____

_____

_____

_____

_____

How can you identify cats?
By looking at a cat-alog

APPOINTMENT SCHEDULE

Time   Date

Veterinarian's name:

Observed cat's problem:

_____

_____

_____

What the veterinarian did:

_____

_____

What the veterinarian said:

_____

_____

_____

Recommendations:

Black as thorn;
Quick as night.
Lovely pharaoh,
In the morning light.

Surging tiger,
Lightning foe.
The path he walks
We'll never know.

—WB

APPOINTMENT SCHEDULE

Time _____ Date _____

Veterinarian's name: _____

Observed cat's problem:

_____

_____

_____

What the veterinarian did:

_____

_____

What the veterinarian said:

_____

_____

_____

Recommendations:

_____

_____

_____

_____

_____

What happens if you are visited by a cat burglar?
Your cat is long gone.

APPOINTMENT SCHEDULE

Time   Date

Veterinarian's name:

Observed cat's problem:

_____

_____

_____

What the veterinarian did:

_____

_____

What the veterinarian said:

_____

_____

_____

Recommendations:

_____

_____

_____   *Sprawling feline at the window lies,*
_____   *What in the great outdoors do you spy?*
                           And would you prefer it
_____   *Raw, boiled, baked or fried?*—WB

♥ ♥ ♥ ♥ Your cat's ♥ ♥ ♥ ♥ medicine record

Here you can record the medicines for your cat

along with directions and recommendations

Date _____ Veterinarian _____

Medicine name _____

Prescribed for the following symptoms _____

_____

_____

Directions for use _____

_____

♥ ♥

Date _____ Veterinarian _____

Medicine name _____

Prescribed for the following symptoms _____

_____

_____

Directions for use _____

_____

Date   Veterinarian

Medicine name

Prescribed for the following symptoms

Directions for use

♥   ♥

Date   Veterinarian

Medicine name

Prescribed for the following symptoms

Directions for use

Date _____ Veterinarian _____

Medicine name _____

Prescribed for the following symptoms _____

_____

_____

_____

Directions for use _____

_____

_____

♥   ♥

Date _____ Veterinarian _____

Medicine name _____

Prescribed for the following symptoms _____

_____

_____

_____

Directions for use _____

_____

*What a
lovely,
wonderful,
perfect,
friendly cat.
What happened to my vase?*

—WB

Your cat's diet

Here you can record the food you order for your cat, the date you purchase it, the amount, the weight (so you can figure out how much your cat eats), and the price.

Date	Food Name	Quantity	Weight	Price

Inoculations
for your cat

Type of shot: _____

Date: _____ Veterinarian: _____

Good for this period of time: _____

Follow up recommended: _____

♥   ♥   ♥   ♥

Type of shot: _____

Date: _____ Veterinarian: _____

Good for this period of time: _____

Follow up recommended: _____

♥   ♥   ♥   ♥

Type of shot: _____

Date: _____ Veterinarian: _____

Good for this period of time: _____

Follow up recommended: _____

♥   ♥   ♥   ♥

Type of shot: _____

Date: _____ Veterinarian: _____

Good for this period of time: _____

Follow up recommended: _____

Type of shot: _____

Date: _____ Veterinarian: _____

Good for this period of time: _____

Follow up recommended: _____

♥　　　♥　　　♥

Type of shot: _____

Date: _____ Veterinarian: _____

Good for this period of time: _____

Follow up recommended: _____

♥　　　♥　　　♥

Type of shot: _____

Date: _____ Veterinarian: _____

Good for this period of time: _____

Follow up recommended: _____

Type of shot: _____

Date: _____ Veterinarian: _____

Good for this period of time: _____

Follow up recommended: _____

Oh, what strange thing,
in the bedroom lies?
He knows it is forbidden,
so what do I spy?

To which any self-respecting cat would reply:
"If you didn't wish to see me in the bedroom,
then why did you turn on the light?—WB*

Cat care record

You can record your feline's care or services here.

This includes shampoos, nail clippings,

and visits to the pet groomers.

Date	Care or Service	Provider	Cost

🐾 Cat family medical history

A medical history of your kitten or cat may be useful in diagnosing future problems. Here's a useful guide to obtaining the information you need.

Date completed

Cat name:

Mother's name   Father's name

Name of parent's owners

Address

City   State   Zip

Telephone number or numbers

Questions to be asked:

Did either parent have any problems? If so, what were they?

What were the symptoms?

*♥ The twilight grew,
with the end of day's light,
The sleek feral hunter,
crouched alone in coming night.
As evening grew stronger,
and day met its death,
he whispered through dark trails,
hunting prey's quiet breath.* —WB

How long did the problem last?
_____

_____

What treatment or treatments relieved the problem?
_____

_____

_____

Vet who treated either parent

Name
_____

Telephone number:
_____

Address
_____

City   State   Zip
_____

Other questions

Is there a general condition you have observed that I should be
aware of or alert to for my cat? What is it?
_____

_____

_____

_____

_____

Any other comments?
_____

_____

Your cat's recurring problems

Write the date and describe the symptoms. Jot down any possible cause that may be behind the problem, such as food, exercise, time of the year, environmental factors, or other related factors. A careful study may give you the clue to the solution.

Date _____ Symptoms _____

_____

What's happening _____

_____

_____

Possible related factors _____

_____

_____

Date _____ Symptoms _____

_____

What's happening _____

_____

Possible related factors _____

_____

_____

*The thing most likely
To drive cats
Close to the edge or over,
Is the invention
Of the silent can opener.*—WB

AGE
AND
YOUR
CAT

How old is your cat in human terms? Though cats age differently than people, a useful comparison between cats and human age is:

Cats	Human Beings
1 year	16 years
3 years	28 years
8 years	48 years
12 years	64 years
15 years	76 years
20 years	96 years

Cats do not age in the same way people do. Most cats enjoy a long middle age and tend to show signs of aging after about 12 years (the equivalent of 64 years in humans.) By the time it is about 15 (a human's 76 years), your cat will spend longer periods of time asleep. Your cat will appear stiff when it moves and will seek heat, because its circulation is poorer.

Cats are longer-lived animals than dogs. There are a number of cats on record who have lived more than 20 years. The maximum recorded life span of a cat was 36 years. Generally speaking, the average life span of a domestic cat is around 15 to18 years.

Love in the morning,
darling at night.
Sweet all his days,
when he doesn't bite.—WB

Warm furry body
in the early morning light.
Sympathetic ear in the evening,
after a hard day's fight.
Oh tiny love,
'tis you who makes things bright.

—WB